ASKING FOR DIRECTIONS

Other Books by Matthew Firth
Suburban Pornography
Shag Carpet Action

ASKING FOR DIRECTIONS

POETRY

MATTHEW FIRTH

anvil
PRESS

Copyright © 2023 by Matthew Firth

All rights reserved. No part of this book may be reproduced by any means without the prior written permission of the publisher, with the exception of brief passages in reviews. Any request for photocopying or other reprographic copying of any part of this book must be directed in writing to Access Copyright: The Canadian Copyright Licensing Agency, Sixty-Nine Yonge Street, Suite 1100, Toronto, Ontario, Canada, M5E 1E5.

Library and Archives Canada Cataloguing in Publication

Title: Asking for directions / Matthew Firth.
Names: Firth, Matthew, 1965- author.
Description: First edition.
Identifiers: Canadiana 20230460577 | ISBN 9781772142181 (softcover)
Subjects: LCGFT: Poetry.
Classification: LCC PS8561.I66 A91 2023 | DDC C811/.54—dc23

Book design by Derek von Esssen
Cover and interior illustrations by Dan Sharp
Represented in Canada by Publishers Group Canada
Distributed by Raincoast Books

The publisher gratefully acknowledges the financial assistance of the Canada Council for the Arts, the Canada Book Fund, and the Province of British Columbia through the BC Arts Council and the Book Publishing Tax Credit.

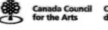 

Anvil Press Publishers Inc.
P.O. Box 3008, Station Terminal
Vancouver, B.C. V6B 3X5 Canada
www.anvilpress.com

PRINTED AND BOUND IN CANADA

For Andrea – now it's poetry

Contents

9 From My Knees
11 How?
12 Poem That Could Get Me Killed in This Country
13 Lost Day
15 Crow
16 It Has Come to This
17 Pileated
18 Getting Sentimental
21 Handyman Nick
23 Psychotherapy
25 Chedoke Creek
26 Fallen Angels
29 Imagining I Can Fly Because I Can
31 Over Oceans
32 Sewing Instructions
33 Widows
35 The Dead
36 Three Days, This Time of Year
38 Quiet Corridors of Lost Love
40 Entropy
41 After the Funeral
43 No One Spoke of Love
44 Little Blue Flowers
45 Erratics
47 1977

Incongruous   48

Chains   49

Heart   50

Heart II   52

My Own Marilyn Monroe   53

Love Poem #22   55

Asking for Directions   57

Geography 451   60

Vital Signs   61

No Cover   62

Fail   64

Throw Your Coats on the Bed   65

M.I.A.   68

Prisoners   70

Unhandy   72

Shoes   73

Blood-red Inks   74

Days Full of Promise   76

Chorus Chants   78

On Restless Days   80

Dead Poet   81

Small Obscure Books   83

Something Else (Poems II)   84

Always Watching   85

FROM MY KNEES

You don't know what poetry is
she said,
as I stared into
her curvy cleavage.
She slurred her words
swirling red wine in a
goblet
too big
for her milky hands. She opened
her mouth again but nothing
came out.

You don't know what poetry is
he said,
as he stabbed a finger at printed words
in an 88-page book coloured with
art by a post-modern paraplegic.
He enunciated his words.
I mean, he *really* enunciated his words.
He gripped that book like a lifeline
veins on his fingers
a shade of rust.

You don't know what poetry is
they said,
so I kept my head on a swivel.
Attackers were everywhere.
I was forced to play defence.
I turned my pockets inside out to
prove I was a pauper.
They relented and took a step back.
Apologized.
I drew

lint from under my fingernails
cursing my artificial beauty.

You, muse – lust of my life.
You, muse – defender of directionless faith.
You, muse – keeper of inner peace.

My heart sputters
knees buckle.
I lie in a bath of my own blood
my semen spilled on thighs
words hard baked
roasted
rotten
completely
utterly
useless
to everyone
but you.

HOW?

How did none of us end up in factories
on shop floors
on road construction crews
or down on our knees banging in carpet?

My granddad lopped off a finger and a half.
An uncle had both legs amputated.
Another died of mesothelioma. My old
man's lungs crystalized and seized
like an old, rusted engine.

Here I sit tap tapping this soft
machine
playing with words
my fingers like dandelions
I once rubbed under my chin.

No one I know drinks rye and Coke.
Sure, we go to football games
drink twelve-dollar beers.
But the stadium – like so many other things – has
been spun on its axis and
I can't tell any more
whether any of this
is real.

POEM THAT COULD GET ME KILLED IN THIS COUNTRY

I feel coming to poetry
this late in life
that I don't have time
to fuck around
with small-timers.
I read dead male
white poets
mostly
Americans.

Cute slim volumes
by cute slim Canadian
up-and-comers
don't move me.
Teach me nothing.
Show me nothing.
I require roily poems written
by dead men who have fallen
out of trees,
blunted and broken their fingers
pulling root vegetables from dry earth
woken up on the wrong
side of the bed.

I am not shut off, nor sleepy.
Rather, I am sharply focused
lasered in on prey.

If I don't kill
I don't eat.
If I don't eat
I could be dead tomorrow.

LOST DAY

Drank whisky
this morning
instead of coffee.
Fell down the stairs at the noon.
There were only three.
A soft landing on the landing.

Scraped my elbow on the
pavement
out front
when my neighbour
pushed me over.
Me – a pushover. We argued
about the rotation of the earth
until it took me in its grip
and brought me to my knees.
A scab will form.

Bathed in honey mustard until
my pores revolted
bowels erupted
teeth ran for the hills.

When all is lost
wrap your arms around something
unmoveable
something
as permanent as we know.
Glacial boulders.
Thousand-year-old trees.
Arsenic.
Mosquito repellent.
Or – your love.

She's right there
where she always is
shelved in a purple pantry (purple panties)
where sacred things
are stored.
Look.
Winter is coming.

CROW

One crow.
Wait for it.
There's always another.

IT HAS COME TO THIS

It turns out
shooting squirrels
in winter
with a slingshot
is trickier than imagined.
Bag of ammo running low.
I've never owned a
bag of ammo
before.
I've only managed
so far
to ping tree branches
bounce shot
off my neighbour's
aluminum siding.

It has come to this.
Shooting at rodents.
Nothing else works.
When the slingshot ammo is gone
I'll step up to a
pellet gun. That is
unless
that fucking grey squirrel
stops doing
fucking grey squirrel things.

Meanwhile, I slowly open
the door to the yard
breathe the sharp winter air
take aim, again.
I have become
the crazy man
on the block.

PILEATED

Even the pimpled boy in the
punk-assed jeans
is moved by the sight of that
big bold bird
hammering away.

He holds out his phone and
thumbs a dozen pics
while weed-clouded friends
loiter and linger.
They look menacing
murderous
until they're not.

We all roll over
and die
eventually.

GETTING SENTIMENTAL

Never jumped off that bridge.
Never hanged myself in shame.
Paid my debts.
Made enemies.
Kept allies close.
Dressed in layers when required.
Walked by the curb so the slop landed on my head.
Made sure she always came hard.
Climbed that mountain nearly naked.
Took my medication.
Memorized the long way home.
Caught grasshoppers barehanded.
Drank from that stream.
Woke up on the wrong side of the bed.
Woke up in unfamiliar places.
Crashed that party.
Took out the head pin in one shot.
Lost my keys.
Found true love.
Flew a kite.
Built a birdhouse out of popsicle sticks.
Piled on.
Raised a fuss.
Raged pointlessly.
Drowned my sorrows.
Danced outside on patio stones.
Killed a few thousand mosquitos.
Visited the infirm.
Mopped floors.
Cleaned toilets.

Stole glances.
Stuck it in.
Played snooker in her basement.
Drove on the wrong side of the road.
Paid for a round.
Taught him to skate and then him.
Wore that suit to that wedding and then that funeral.
Typed out clear instructions.
Painted the garage.
Decorated a few dozen Christmas trees.
Let my hair grow long and then let it down.
Took the elevator to the top.
Stayed out of ditches and quarries.
Never switch hit.
Sang along to a thousand songs, probably more.
Walked quietly by the river listening to the ice.
Took advice from old women.
Never bought anything from a gypsy.
Changed trains in Toronto.
Shovelled snow for the neighbours.
Gave away spare change.
Dressed in rags.
Played that part.
Ate that oyster.
Stared into the sun.
Wondered why.

My list – incomplete
to this point.
I will add more.

HANDYMAN NICK

He stands in my basement holding
my son's hockey stick, leaning on it, testing
the flex, like he knows what he's
doing.
He's a right shot.
My son is a left but
this does not deter him.
"I had a tryout," he says.
"With the 67s."
I look at him and let him talk.
"I was small but those fuckers
couldn't catch me, at least not on the
first day."
I sip my coffee and listen.
"Too quick until fucking
Potvin catches me with an elbow in
a scrimmage. That was it. Game over. *Finito!*"
He flicks his wrists, scraping the stick's
wrong-handed blade along the cement,
shooting an imaginary
puck.
"That right?" I say. "That really sucks."
He feigns some kind of dipsy-doodle,
then leans the stick
back against the wall. Straightens
his ballcap.
Sighs.

I wish he'd get back to work,
finish the tiling
and then
get the hell
out of my house
instead of regaling
me with his old-timer shit.
But I give him his moment.
He sighs again and droops
his shoulders.
I sip my coffee
wait for it to happen.

PSYCHOTHERAPY

When the river fully freezes over
it starts to sing.
It's not a lament or murder ballad.
Under the crystal green sun
there are no sad songs.
There is only peace,
finally.
Peace imprisoned beneath the ice.

My black brain bounces
off jail-cell bars
crying out for attention.
Quiet now.
Hush.
Shsssh.
It's here.
Crouch down beside me
listen to the river's freedom song.

CHEDOKE CREEK

We caught salamanders in bare hands
tadpoles in aluminum pie plates.
Before the City put up a grate
we went underground
where the creek met the sewer system.
With flashlights
we scurried all the way to Aberdeen Avenue
looked up at passing cars.
Rats lived there.
We saw their black shadows.
Our walk back to daylight took longer.

In spring, we once saw a porcupine
in the elbow of a tree.
West of the creek, through to the edge of the woods,
we rummaged for golf balls
by the 15th fairway.

Later, having stashed mickeys of rum
under fallen trees and dead leaves,
we always found them before
parties and dances.
Drunk on half a bottle,
we stupidly smashed
glass where once we played.
We had new catches on our minds.
Chased teenaged girls.
We were in love with their warm breath
their firm breasts
that grew larger every summer.

FALLEN ANGELS

I recognize him by his gait
and the enormous size of his head.
Last time I saw him
we played road hockey on
Undercliff Avenue.
Peter Stinson.
His father, I remember, was a lawyer.
What is Peter doing on Yonge Street
looking tired beaten down
decades later
10pm on a Tuesday?

In the Zanzibar
I tip the doorman five dollars
pay fourteen dollars for a can of beer
tip the stripper with the tiny tits
six dollars as she
sets the sweating can
on the wobbly table
where I sit.
Watch the floor show.
Watch guys thirty years younger
pay fifty dollars for a table dance.
Hit the pavement
defeated confused.

In a green grocer's
I repent for my sins
rubbing blood oranges on open wounds.
This costs extra.
Jerk chicken.
Tofu samosas.
Limes lemons white grapefruit.
Wash it down with a litre of chocolate milk
two days from final expiration.

In the hotel lobby
elevator corridor
I chase rabbits squirrels
sing with song sparrows
dance with Florida panthers.
Dirty dishes stacked outside
my door.
Fancy fob fallen to the floor.
Do Not Disturb door display.
This is not my room.
A naked man explodes into space
kicking cold pizza crusts my way.
I realize, then:
wrong floor wrong time wrong life.

In the street
thirty-five floors below
Peter Stinson from Undercliff disappears
underground riding the subway
to the end of time.
The barman counts out tips
to tiny-titted strippers
in slippers
wiping away blotted mascara
drying their tears with
filthy blankets.
Their gyrations have ceased.
The clerk in the 24-hour green grocer's
faces-up tins of syrupy peaches at 3am.
I sleep by a hotel room window that
will not open
in a city that is not my mistress –
wasted hours eroded hearts misapplied dreams of love
fallen angels
everywhere.

IMAGINING I CAN FLY BECAUSE I CAN

I dropped out.
Walked away.
Left that report unwritten
that task undone
that binder full of
misdirected energy
sitting on my desk
beside the highway.

I'm not judging you
but how can that email
that message
that phone call
hold as much promise
as the flight of that small
bird from branch
to brook
from seed to sand?

I fall to my knees and wail
at the shores of the lapping river.
Take me with you.
There's got to be something better.

There, in the reflection:
a new light.
Eyes shine brightly from birth
to death.
Your skin might crease and crow
but that glow comes
from wonderment and woe.
Drop everything.
Run with me into the sunset.
Float with me six feet above the ground.
Drink it in.
Dance.
There's so much more
to be done
together.

OVER OCEANS

Stayed up too late searching
for glimpses of my son in Vancouver.
Woke with a cough on a creaky bed.

I have scars on my heart
from too much sunshine.
I portion affection
in tablespoons
count backwards
remember when the dead
were carried on shoulders
then launched like paper airplanes
made from Sunday leftovers.

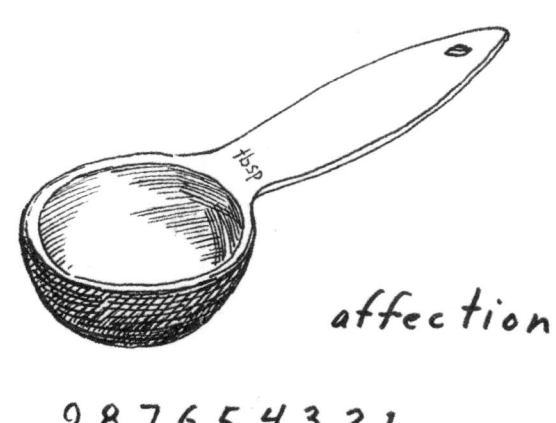

SEWING INSTRUCTIONS

How does that bird
light as a thimble
flit chirp and fly
at minus twenty degrees
while we're stuck down here
jabbing ourselves
like pincushions
frozen in fear?
Such beautiful singers.
There is something to learn here.

WIDOWS

I made the mistake of getting a job
loving a woman
not blowing my paycheques
not developing a habit.

I did the unthinkable when I had two kids
paid my rent
didn't get arrested
didn't fuck her sister.

I clearly messed up when I made money for these boots
listened to advice
didn't fall down drunk
showed up on time.

Build your own myth and blend it with
fragments of your shattered dreams.
I'll write these poems on the train or
this laptop or
on my back deck by bird feeders
I paid for.

Who cares if you claim street cred
pain suffering
abuse at the hands of low-level tyrants.
It doesn't change the fact
you cannot dance
worth a good
god damn.

Your yellow teeth
yellow hair
bachelor apartment fallen arches
puckered lips
they're more contaminated than the end
of my tongue licking this new envelope
mailing fabled reconstructions
instead of letter-bombs and threats.

Let's make a pact and stop identifying
with albatross silence
and by this I mean shit.

None of what you say
none of what I write
is true.
Full stop.

THE DEAD

We've got it all wrong.
The dead don't drift
up to heaven or
pitch down to Hell.
The dead
settle like dust motes
on stones sweetgrass
asphalt
then scatter in every
direction
the heaviest
no heavier
than a song sparrow's broken
heart.

THREE DAYS, THIS TIME OF YEAR

Christmas Eve
after an outdoor skate
I soak in the bath
with a beer and a book.
My heart slows and sputters
as I slide
into hot steamy water.
They will cut me open some time
next year but that's a million
miles away just now.

Christmas Day brings freezing rain
hot coffee sleepy
heads. The retreat
deepens with the first morning
light coffee birds and ghosts
on the radio.

Boxing Day brings snow I
brush from eyebrows
kick from my boots
soldiering through fields to the
frozen river. Across the ice
faint light strikes ancient rock and
my adoration for you grows more rigid
in shape and form.
Decades ago
you gave me your phone number
scrawled on a scrap
of red wrapping paper.
Later, I tattooed your initials
on my arm.

Now, fearing that that's not enough,
I'll ask that your initials
be carved on my open heart
when the surgery is over.
A quick scalpel flick and
my mended flesh will resemble
a whittled tree
picnic table
a symbol
another part of you
scored etched lacerated
inside me.

QUIET CORRIDORS OF LOST LOVE

She collects her trauma in a change purse
unclasps it
counts out pain carefully, slowly –
three-thousand pennies paid
for a dozen stale pastries.

Reading by the sleeping dog
I catch his contagious somnolence.
Soporific breathing draws me in.
I lapse for three minutes
before jerking awake
still on page 39.

In the concrete curbing in front
of the house where I grew up
an iron loop hangs rusted. Years before
the iceman
tied his horse here.
In 1973 I clang that hitching loop up and down
back and forth
as July heat hammers down on my small, brown hands.
I have nowhere to be this afternoon. It is just
me, this iron relic, furious black ants on the sidewalk,
and my cute neighbour in saddle shoes who smiles
just for me – another story I tell myself.

Over Styrofoamed coffee in the parish hall
my mother tells the minister his choice of hymns
this morning was grand. No choir any more, she is not
deterred. A single voice praising the Lord.
All the harps in heaven join her, support her,
lift her unto her maker. After hearing this, I melt sugar cubes
on my tongue and chase the Sunday school girls out the door.

I love the way
their skirts sway.

Our black rotary telephone
could not be outdone.
Cordless wireless mobile cellular smart.
It was none of these things but its
weight in your hand felt like purpose.
Do you remember waiting for the phone to ring
Saturday nights?
We stole our dads' beer
smashed empties in the woods
ran from police
hid in bowling alleys
laughed until morning
shrugged off hangovers
did it all again.

Now, melting snow
meets the hastened silence
of your words.
Your sleeping body is draped
across the globe
reminding me of a deer trail
broken through tall grass.

She unclasps her change purse once more.
Counts out pain in pennies.
Takes the time she needs.

A dozen stale pastries in
quiet corridors of lost love.

ENTROPY

This poem is written in
Calibri (Body) 11-point text
not because a 16th century
poet scripted
verse this way
but because it is this
machine's default
and I've never bothered
to change it, not sure
I know how.

I can show you
one thousand other
things like this.
Butternuts and birds.
Cracked curbing at my feet.
The disintegration of time and the slow
running away of my faith
in anything other than
warm touch
at the altar
of your hips.

AFTER THE FUNERAL

We drove straight through the night.
Left in darkness
listening to Australian programming
rebroadcast on the CBC.
Arrived in early daylight
before traffic reporters ruined the trip.

We should have left the day before
but heavy snow made driving impossible.
The trains fully booked.
Flying out of the question.

Straight to the rented house for a couple hours sleep.
Then cleaned up and put on our Sunday best.
Dutifully took our places among the mourners.
Afterward, the church basement crowded
with family friends miniature sandwiches
watered-down coffee.

Back at the house
family ate chili
pulled bottles of beer from a case of twenty-four.
Apple pie. Cherry cheesecake. Butter tarts with raisins.
Euchre over a bottle of Canadian Club.

Later we told stories recalled memories
myths
while kids dozed on sofas and
blankets by the fireplace.

Friends arrived after midnight.
Lubricated conversation swerved to current affairs history politics
– even art –
until the last guest walked away drunk around 4 a.m..

Upstairs in an unfamiliar bed my cock stiffened in your
hand, as it has a thousand times before.
Death brought us here.
It seemed right to fuck it away
until a new sun
crowned in the east.

NO ONE SPOKE OF LOVE

We started to take our meals in
bright blue bowls.
Pulled the curtains closed and
tucked our feet away.

Outside: gunshots and fallen warriors.
A yellow haze slung low over the city.
Dead rabbits and
abject failure.

It was quieter under the mountain
where we
could finally breathe, where
no one spoke of love.

LITTLE BLUE FLOWERS

You lose touch, drift.
Put things off, procrastinate.
You set intentions that
fester unfulfilled.

A flower blooms and you remember her.
You last saw her
in a grocery store
near the frozen foods.
She did not look good; pale, gaunt.
A jolt but you pushed optimism on her
for five minutes.

You tell me this morning the flower is called
Forget Me Not.
It lives up to its name
that little blue beauty.

We sit a while longer, waiting for the day
to shift move tilt
any which way.
After a pause,
"She's likely been dead ten years," I say.
"Her kids were what, 8 and 10 at the time?"

We sit among the flowers.
Around us
spring slides suddenly into steamy summer
calendars unclutter
and just beyond our reach
hope crests
and then dies
alone.

ERRATICS

We walked past light rail construction
an abandoned
Japanese restaurant
cross-country skiers
a partially frozen river
bold chickadees flying within
arm's reach
heritage beach homes
dog walkers
games of shinny out on the lake
a murmuration of starlings.

Conversation rambled from
topic to topic but
settled and then lingered on
one giant boulder
tagged with graffiti.
One rock two metres
tall and wider across.
You said these rocks have a specific
geological name
but you could not remember it.
A mile-high glacier dragged
and scattered this rock that now
lies cut off from its kind.

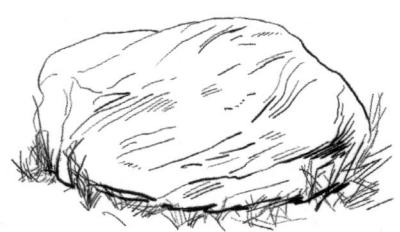

Later, it came to you: "Erratics".
You sent me the name by text, just the one
word
alone.
I am tempted to
turn philosophical, both
about the name of the rock
and its relationship
to our lives.
I won't.
I'll only concede
that I wonder about our random walks
how many more we'll take.
Or who I'll walk with when I'm 75.
Or whether I'll be walking
at all at that age.
We could both be dead.
And if a walk doesn't
happen, does anyone notice?
When I'm 75, that rock might have had its graffiti
scrubbed clean or
painted over
or more likely it
will sit there still alone
unaffected
its proper name
forgotten. A rock is a
rock.
A walk, a
walk.

1977

The girls have always failed to notice.

Pantry shelves are masked
by an old flannel sheet.
Milk bags washed,
hung to dry. They will be re-used.

There is a growing
myth of my brown eyes attracting anything
but a new version of
mismanaged awards and errors.

Forty years later
the dying sun blisters my skin.
All the Sheilas
Catherines
Rachels
and Donnas
drunkenly row their tiny boats
in circles on a choppy lake.
Thunderclouds. Ravens.
No-name baked beans in salty sauce.
The curtain
comes down, slowly for some,
suddenly for others.
We do not get to
choose when or how.

Sheila Catherine Rachel Donna –
meet me under the glue-sniffing bleachers
for one last touch of your golden robes
before this experiment
fails again.

INCONGRUOUS

Iced-over windows
cold blue hearts.
The man in the purple hat
kicks tires
measures his faults
and foibles, then
turns away
losing purchase.
Drunk monkeys raid the party.
The rainy season is coming.
Here, let me help you with that.

CHAINS

I put chains on my hands
to crawl over mountains.
I am blinded by a black star.

I found my train in Chicago.
We pushed west in a driving rain.
Awoke in Iowa
pulled maps up to my chin
the thinnest of ratty blankets.
I am not a traveller
nor a survivor.

Fresh blood on your hands
between my gums
under our fingernails
in the crooks behind your knees.
Knees you fall to
before clawing at the old earth
that won't
have you,
yet.

HEART

Shirt off.
Wires stuck to me with stickies.
Tucked into a foetal position.
The technician does a reach-around
with her device.
I hear my heart
through her greased mechanical probe
muffled thumping that sounds
slushy distant precarious.

I also hear it when I
shovel snow
climb stairs too quickly.
When I'm balls deep inside you.

It's powered by the pomegranates
I eat for breakfast.
You in
red panties.
Osprey. Kindness.
Three-point shots smiling sons.

She's got heart.
He's got heart.
I've got heart.

Cut me open.
I cringe seeing red muscle white tendon
blue sinew raw brown blood.

It's better not to listen.
Trust the beat.
Close your eyes, try to sleep.
Let her work that clucking machine
take her pictures
look for calcified flaws.
Yes, flaws.

My heart limps
tripping over fallen branches
stumbling over slumped dreams.
I careen toward
a flat-lined horizon
where bird skeletons
skim fluttering waves.

Before then: listen, to everything.
Let it all race murmur skip bleat beat.
And then – press in next
to yours
until we both
explode.

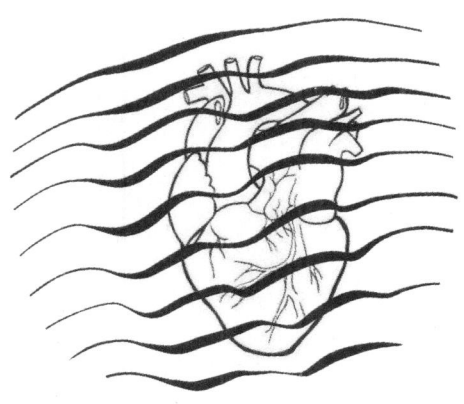

HEART II

In bed
last night
I came up for air
and felt it
before I heard it.
My heart vibrating trilling thumping
pounding behind my ribs.
Speeding.
Racing.
Running.
Echoing.

Swept my left hand over
your right hip
looked down at the way your
back arced.
Thought about death
my death
even though I was – in that moment –
electrically
mythically
hyperbolically
very much
alive.

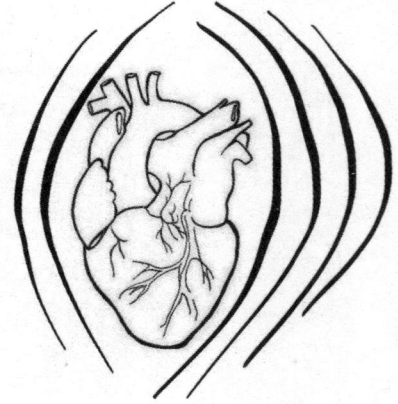

MY OWN MARILYN MONROE

You were camera shy
that day
on a cement pier in
Port Dover
refused to be
photographed in
a brilliant red bikini.
Instead, we ate foot-long hotdogs
as Lake Erie's waves
broke furiously
at your feet.

Rather than a black limousine
we arrived at a boutique hotel
in Manhattan by yellow cab.
Still, the doorman did
his job.
You stepped into a slice of
afternoon sunshine
cutting through
a corridor of 60-storey
towers
illuminating your arrival.

I'd never considered
the benefits of a proper Champagne
glass. Or flute, if
we're going to get
technical.
But watching those bubbles
rise toward your lips
as your
right hand held the stem

made me curse
my fallow breeding,
before falling at your feet
an unholy supplicant.

I can't hit like DiMaggio
or write like Miller
but you still see beauty in
my faults
shortcomings.
It takes a simple
sincere apology
and all is forgiven
before we start again.

I watched your hairstyle change
new colours both
natural and not
various lengths
permutations.
High-heeled shoes or barefoot
your best
black dress for Saturday night
or tousled and naked in bed on
Sunday morning in an overheated
hotel room.
I watched you
cultivate novelty
year after year
stocking my mind with a
million confidential
glamour
shots.

LOVE POEM #22

There is a quiet
morning moment
before the rest of the world
staggers stumbles
and plods
back to what
we call life
when I
bottle the silence
hold the stillness
stop the movement
of time
linger in this space
with a cup of coffee
that does not cool
waiting for you
to walk into the
room barefoot
while nothing
else shifts moves rumbles
or
even exists
at all.

ASKING FOR DIRECTIONS

In bed
she said
get off the sideroads
and pay more attention.
That'll get us both where
we want to go
sooner
rather than later.

Looks like a postcard today
bright sunshine
fresh snow on cedar hedges rabbit prints.
I hear the furnace hum
not the wailing moans of dying neighbours.

My dad's surveyor's tape measure is
marked only in inches.
If you want to know feet
get off your duff
and do the math.

Becoming aware of my faltering stability
I approach any incline cautiously
my ass
ready to absorb
any fall from grace.

What did that dream mean where
I was a clerk
working in a sporting good store with football
players shackled and strung up by their
wrists above the store's front door? That can't
be good for business.
I was so troubled by the imagery
I tried walking it off at 4 a.m.
pacing laps in
my living room
like a polar bear in a zoo.

I've never had to deal with avalanche warnings.
The map of the valley had to be
redrawn after three landslides
wiped out the village. On the road
up the escarpment, I often pondered
those "Falling Rock Zone" signposts
gazing at sedimentary rock
its apparent precariousness.

She knows her way around the kitchen
the dance floor the bedroom but
can't tell north from south to save her
soul.

With a telescope this powerful
I can peer into your veins and arteries
through silk curtains
penetrate cinderblock hearts.
Simply put
I see what you're hiding.

Meet me at the parade
next to the Kool-Aid stand
by the pretty girl handing out free condoms
and the guy on stilts who never
comes down to earth.
We'll clap and dance until one of us
ends up truly fucked.

What compels those butterflies
to migrate when the slightest breeze knocks them
off the pussy willows
straight into rush-hour traffic?

Sometimes it's best to stay put.
Or walk the route you know too well.
Other times break trails
tamp down obstruction and
run with the panicked frenzy
of a million gazelles,
faster than everything
that wants us dead.

GEOGRAPHY 451

Africa is a warped upside-down gourd
segmented into colours:
orange blue purple pink.
Mauritania appears as a shade of lavender
while further north
Alaska looks cancerous
brown lumpy distended
growing out of Canada's right shoulder.

In my group
Greg lives a few blocks east
wisecracking Jim buses in from beyond city limits
Vivian's family moved north
from Dominica, coloured red,
if you can find it in an atlas.

To the west
our teacher leans over
hardworking immigrant
girls moved here from across the globe.
He peeks down their blouses
at new landmasses rising.

VITAL SIGNS

Full moon over your shoulder
on the coldest night of the year.

My heart still works
so please don't die before I do.
I won't eat drink wash
sleep.
Not out of laziness
or resignation
or old-school gender roles.
I'll just be
lost
all sense of direction
leaking out of me
staining the pavement
where once we walked.

I've got a different narrative in my head
where I turn cold
then flit and fly around
reminding you
where you left your phone
when the laundry should come in off the line
when to walk the dog.

You'll hold me
under your skin
inside out
a new vital organ
that works for you
alone.

NO COVER

Night out.
Relatively dressed up.
Reasonably priced beer.
Old timers on stage.

The woman to our left takes out her pencil crayons
draws a remarkable likeness
of the man sitting behind
wearing a faded fedora.
She hands that likeness
to him
on her
way outside for a smoke.
He holds it limply
wondering – I imagine –
how he got to look
that old.
Grey hair too long.
Beard scrappy.
Collar flaccid.
Shoulders sagged.
He doesn't realize
that at the very least
he should pay for her
next
round.

You are not impressed.
You wait for him to step to the can
then you take that illustrated likeness
tack it to the wall
where drunks throw darts
and dreams slide into salted streets.

Next, you lead
me to the dance floor.
There
my hands
find your fluid hips.
I hold on.
Close my eyes.
Move and
feel it.

FAIL

We named my granddad's
crab apple tree branches
for all the planets.
At six
I fell into the raspberry bushes
on failed mission to
Pluto.

THROW YOUR COATS ON THE BED

Blanched and kale are two words
I heard together for the first time just a few
years ago.

Time tilts, space shifts.
Fish sticks.
Creamed corn.
Pork and beans.
Tinned peaches in syrup.

Stuff your gloves into your
toque
jam your toque into your coat sleeve
then throw your coat on
the double bed with all the others.
Porcelain black baby looks pensive.
Meet us in the rec room.

Bob and Shirley were
euchre-night regulars.
The other couples I can't remember.
Two card tables.
Eight folding chairs.
Clean ashtrays set out.
Bottles of rye gin rum on
the kitchen counter.
Mix.
Bucket full of ice.
Beer in the basement fridge
I was sent to
fetch.
11pm the living room
thick with hazy smoke

drunken laughter exclamations
over cards laid
and cards played.
Later, everyone shuffled into metal-clad
V8s
and
drove
home
hammered.

In a southern Ontario landfill
there's a winter coat of mine that will
not decay
with a zipper that would still work
perfectly were that coat
exhumed.
But this fucking coat – *this* coat I wear now –
that's all of four years old and
purchased not at Kresge's or Bi-way
but at some chi-chi outfitters in
Westboro – has a zipper
that catches
gums
brings me to the brink
of crime
at least twenty times a winter.

A weight presses down
now that both my
father and mother are
dead.

The old man left school at
17 and worked steadily
for the next 44 years

until circumstances changed.
He retired having never
turned on a computer.
Died without email
but – Christ – did he know a double-suited
lone hand
when he saw one.

Strawberries were boiled
with bleached white sugar
then fed into a dented
stainless-steel colander
pounded and thinned with a wooden pestle.
Jam seeped out.
Poured it into old Mason and Gerber jars
sealed with wax.

I have no choice
but to assume this mantle.

I see him in my hands when they
ache on cold mornings.
I see her when
a task's urgency cannot be explained
just
completed.

Fish sticks.
Creamed corn.
Pork and beans.
Tinned peaches in syrup.
And now, blanched kale.

There seems no end to any of this.

M.I.A.

I deserted the war.
Walked away from the rancour and rubble
pushing an old wooden wheelbarrow
holding trace amounts of my imagination.
Three miles down the road
I overturned that wheelbarrow
dumping its contents into a fetid culvert.
There, my best ideas
my disjointed and
hyperbolic thoughts
roiled in
the slow current
seeking a route to sea.

Later, I burned the wheelbarrow on
a beach, sleeping alone under
the starless murk.
Morning brought fog.
Morning brought nothing to eat.
Christ's apparition loomed above the waves.
No one really walks on water.
I thought I'd drown but music
arrived and I started to swim.

Cresting serpents escorted me safely
to an island.
I built a cabin from elephant bones.
The fog lifted.
I worked.
Ate corn and crumpets
until I died
loved and alone.

My washed-out dreams
lapped in the shallows
by the shoreline.

PRISONERS

Shaved my balls
on the coldest day of the year.
Grew a beard in the middle
of summer.
Hollered at a stranger
in the park
armed with blue green red
disks thrown
too close to my head.
He was practising something.
Called him an asshole from one-hundred metres
away.
Doubt he heard but he hollered back something
garbled.
Let it drop.
No fight today.
Exited the park.
Climbed chain-link fences.
Chased balls into the street.
Pried open catch-basin covers.
Threw snowballs at bus windows.
Jumped hedges.
Slid down ravines.
Broke windows.

Smashed bottles
and eventually soaked my shoes
in a pitch-black creek
panning for fool's gold
in a city
with purple-grey air
cheap emerald prostitutes
swerving invalids
men in green-patch safety boots
drunk on rye whisky
pulling their best punches
stuck inside their poisoned paddocks.

UNHANDY

I have no half-finished basement projects.
The garage is not a place where I retreat
to tinker.
The lawn garden hedges
are independent, taking care
of themselves.
Yes, I shovel snow.
Take bins to the curbing and bring
them back.
Hang laundry to dry.
Shuffle and rearrange deckchairs
while slowly sinking.
I will leave nothing behind
but these words
scribbled on scraps of paper
flawed memories
my scent souring on
your soft skin.

SHOES

Say less, write less. You will
be heard
more.

Out near the farm the train whistle blows
holding our heads under water
drowning all our thoughts. Up we come
for air, before
gathering and staring at our shoes,
silent.

Some of us leaving, others
arriving.

BLOOD-RED INKS

The poets have stormed
the suburbs
taken their show
on the road
to strip malls box stores empty transit stations.

Downtown
dusty artists
discombobulated queers and queens
search for car keys phones wallets.

Uptown
lawyers and investment
bankers fly kites beneath
crumbling hotels
while hookers johns
and janes demand their life savings in small
unmarked bills.

Midtown is all grey gosling traffic
dead puffins rotting in the gutter.

Nothing is as it seems.

Around the corner and up
the hill, a man leans over his
balcony in mid-December bellowing the
works of Dostoyevsky at inattentive titmice. The birds
don't sing back. They fly away
and shit on
old stone
husbands.

Back here
it's peaches and cream. Lattes
and ancient Irish whiskies.
Coyotes
wander the streets at night feasting on
our neglected young. I see their bones
piled neatly
curbside
every morning when
I emerge at daybreak
eager to lick road salt
off your bare and brazen stomach.

Is this how it ends?

No, the storm passes. Skies clear.
Poets wake late in the day.
And – as they do –
write it all down in
bold and
blood-red inks.

DAYS FULL OF PROMISE

Will they start arresting poets again and
banish them deep in cold forests
to suppress their thoughts
and words?
Or have they learned new tricks
and put them on the payroll?
How are protest singers supposed to
spread their gospel when the rails
have been removed? I haven't been lately
but don't I remember seeing hobos
in airports drinking eight-dollar coffees.
Hip-hoppers won't save us.
Hackers won't save us.
Influencers want your ego and your likes.

Prophets stand naked in the desert.
A trillion grains of sand are just that:
rock fragmented in this universe I'm told
is thirteen billion years old
but existed before then
in a form none of us can
imagine,
"before then" being
a useless descriptor.

Write me a letter expressing rage
and discomfort.
Drop it in the mail.
I'll get it 3-5 days later
and rub your words
into holes
in my old jeans
thinking
back to drunk days
full of promise
when none of us were
young
and all of us were blind.

CHORUS CHANTS

Put on this earth to be blamed
I retreat to the furthest corners of the meadow.

The dog cries outside the latched door
unable to accept her departure.

The forest is open to spectators
who must scrub graffiti from painted trees.

The river iced over in August
holding each of us responsible for its pain.

I'm in love with the winged woman
dive bombing from your balcony.

Stepping off the train in Cincinnati
she falls to her knees to pray for peace.

If the cow jumps over the moon
who will clean up its mess?

Molly projects revenue increases over the next quarter
while her nurse changes the dressing on seeping wounds.

Told that the changes are only temporary
the man in the blue hat asked for an annulment.

On days this cold in this city by the river
I often wonder when we'll stop talking about the oppressed.

White men hold up giant fish for the camera
ignoring hurricane-force winds blowing in from their love lockets.

He turned cold to the touch in just a few minutes
there's not enough whisky in Spain to settle this argument.

Her bad skin doesn't conceal imagined pain
false memories left out too long are rotten to the core.

When Darryl raised his sixth of the casket
we all felt the strain of the cold ceiling joists pop.

Housebound and vainglorious
we were eager to dance at the Legion until well past eleven.

Todd took the wheel of the truck at that critical moment
and Gerry brought the house down with ordinary magic.

In the darkest corners of the basement
the cogs that drive the engine seized with saltwater tears.

This can't go on forever, she said
holding a damp towel to her open sores.

ON RESTLESS DAYS

I pitch twist twitch.
I read history to think.
Poetry makes me write.
Other days, I throw my books in the river
climb atop
your song.
From up here, I can almost
see you bleed.

DEAD POET

Dreamt I was at a suicide's funeral.
On a canvas tarp
we hoisted him overhead.
He lay there like some kind of
droopy piñata.
Blindfolded we took our best shot
trying to crack him open.
The faithful
the curious
watched and applauded.
We drank to gods
that never existed
before falling
Humpty Dumpty-like
into the arms of
lost loves.

No miracles were performed.
No light shone forth from
orifice or channel.

Awake
startled
unnerved –
I reached out in the dim
morning light
and crawled
inside your
fenced-in heart.

SMALL, OBSCURE BOOKS

Dan and I stood two metres
apart in the cold. We talked about
the dead poet.
Dan was his friend, me
an acquaintance.

He handed me some of the poet's books, sharing history.
I took the books and glanced at their covers, then stared
into the quiet
tree nearby and thought:
How much longer?
How much longer
until we, too, are
history, until we, too, are remembered
– if at all –
in small, obscure books?

SOMETHING ELSE (POEMS II)

The best poems
I've read
are those I
can't recall.
I got lost
drifted
thinking – instead – about
groceries schoolyard fights blow jobs
weight-training regimens bills to be paid
debts to be collected friends to thank for their loyalty
trips to the dentist my wife dressed in anything black and tight
and on it went
until
I circled back
or
moved on to
something else
entirely.

ALWAYS WATCHING

Late winter
in the woods out near Calabogie
looking for owls.
Yes, owls.

Four hours on snow-packed trails.
Nothing but
nuthatches
chickadees
pileated woodpecker destruction.
Stop to piss behind a tree,
see it:
decapitated chipmunk
fur knotted
twisted eviscerated
tiny ribs scored and exposed.
No owls – just owl litter.

Later, over beers,
surrounded by snowmobilers
at the Redneck Bistro
by a still-frozen lake
I look for and find
your heart
served
raw
on a porcelain platter
garnished
with
fading
late-March daylight.

Acknowledgments

Thank you Brian Kaufman and Anvil Press for seamlessly holding your faith as I swerved from fiction to poetry.

Thank you Bill Brown for walking, talking shop, advising me on how to make these poems glow.

Thank you Dan Sharp for bolstering these words with your wonderful illustrations and for being an early-morning and late-night hockey pal.

Thank you Andrea, Sam and Willem for helping me turn, bloom, and occasionally smile.

MATTHEW FIRTH lives in Ottawa. He doesn't divide his time in any other city or town. He lives a life centred on love, lacrosse, beer, books, old-timers hockey, community, and family. He is the author of four short story collections, including *Shag Carpet Action* and *Suburban Pornography* (also both published by Anvil Press). He is a regular contributor to *subTerrain*, where he writes the ever-softening column Crank n File. *Asking for Directions* is his first full-length collection of poems.